Cooking in Season

Making the most of your weekly farm basket

For Xavier,

with affection

Connie Dorval

Connie

The inspiration behind this book is, of course, the beautiful food raised at Field 51 Produce in Goshen, Ky. Working with farmer Dave Keal and my sister farmhands Elizabeth, Diane and Margaret over several seasons has been a joy. The recipes in this book are compiled from all the weekly recipes I provided for our CSA members, in hopes they would not be discouraged by the sometimes staggering amount of fresh produce that made its way into their baskets each week.

CONTENTS

BY THE SEASON:

For a complete listing of all 100 recipes by main ingredient, refer to the Index on page 79.

Chapter 1

First things first:
Greens, greens, greens

If you aren't Southern, or didn't grow up eating greens, a CSA basket can be challenging. The early weeks of the season are heavy on greens – something many of us have only come to love as grown-ups. And if you haven't found the love yet, now's the time! Here are some recipes to consider for your first few baskets. And remember: Many basket items will repeat throughout the season.

Arugula – it's not just for salads

Arugula can be an acquired taste, especially if it is peppery. For me, the spicier the better – I love to eat it in a salad with a few walnuts, a sprinkle of bleu or goat cheese, and some chopped apple or pear. But for some people, it may be just a little too spicy to eat on its own, so here are a few ideas for you to try.

Warm White Bean and Arugula Salad
(With crusty bread, a nice, light supper)

2 slices bacon, crispy and crumbled (optional)
Olive oil
½ cup finely chopped onion
2 cloves garlic, minced
1 can white beans, rinsed
Splash of chicken or vegetable broth
Juice of one lemon
A little chopped fresh parsley
Salt and pepper to taste
Arugula

Heat a skillet to medium-low; add a good drizzle of olive oil, then add in the onion and garlic, stirring for a few minutes until softened. Stir in the beans, add a splash of broth, and cook, stirring gently, until heated through. Add in the lemon juice, parsley and seasonings and mix. Put the arugula in a big bowl, add the bean mixture and toss to coat. Sprinkle with the bacon crumbles, if you are using. The warmth of the bean mixture takes some of the "pepper" out of the arugula. Delicious.

Fabulous Grilled Cheese and Arugula Sandwich
This is just about the most delicious sandwich around. I have tried it with various cheeses, and it's always yummy.

Good whole wheat bread
Fresh arugula
Gruyere or other similar cheese, sliced
Kalamata mayonnaise (mix chopped kalamata olives with mayonnaise)

Spread some kalamata mayo on both pieces of bread; place a layer of cheese and arugula; butter the outsides of the bread and toast in a skillet until golden brown and the cheese is melted. Divine.

Arugula and Tatsoi Salad with Honey-Ginger Dressing

Fresh arugula and tatsoi (enough for your family)
Thin slices of red onion, to your taste
A handful of chopped walnuts or pepitas
Salt and pepper, as needed

Tear the greens into bite-sized pieces, mix all ingredients in salad bowl, toss with Honey-Ginger dressing and season with S&P as needed.

Honey-Ginger dressing (amounts approximate)
1 cup olive oil
¼ cup soy sauce or Bragg's amino acids
1 lemon or 2 limes, juiced
3 cloves garlic, minced
2-3 T. fresh ginger root, peeled and grated
1 T. honey
1 tsp. Dijon mustard
Freshly ground black pepper, to taste

Whisk together all the dressing ingredients except for the oil. When the ingredients are well mixed, taste a smidge – if you like it a little sweeter, whisk in a little more honey or a pinch of sugar. Then add the oil in a steady stream and keep on whisking until all the oil is added and nicely blended. Store in a glass jar in the fridge.

Arugula Pesto

½ cup of shelled walnuts
2 cups of packed arugula leaves, stems removed
4 - 6 garlic cloves
½ cup fresh Parmesan cheese
½ tsp. salt
½ cup extra virgin olive oil

Lightly toast the nuts in a pan over medium heat until lightly brown; let cool for a few minutes. In a food processor or blender, combine all ingredients and process until smooth. Adjust seasonings to taste – how spicy the arugula is will determine the flavor. Serve with pasta, over roasted potatoes, as a sauce for pizza, or as a sandwich spread. Fabuloso.

Linguine with Arugula, Pine Nuts and Parmesan
Serves 6

1 lb. linguine
½ cup olive oil
4 oz. arugula, trimmed
1 cup grated Parmesan cheese
1 cup pine nuts, toasted
Additional Parmesan cheese for serving

Cook linguine in large pot of boiling salted water until just tender but still firm to bite, stirring occasionally. Meanwhile, heat oil in heavy large skillet over medium heat. Add arugula and stir until just wilted, about 30 seconds. Remove from heat.

Drain pasta and return to pot. Add arugula and toss well. Add 1 cup Parmesan and salt and pepper to taste; toss well. Transfer to bowl. Sprinkle with pine nuts. Serve immediately, passing additional Parmesan separately.

Arugula Corn Salad with Bacon
Serves 4

3 cups of cooked and cooled corn kernels (about 4 ears)
2 cups of chopped arugula
4 strips of bacon, cooked, chopped
1/3 cup chopped green onions
1 T. olive oil
1 T. wine vinegar
1/8 tsp. ground cumin
Salt and freshly ground black pepper to taste

Mix together corn, chopped arugula, bacon and onions. In a separate bowl, whisk together the oil, vinegar, salt and pepper, and cumin, pour onto salad and toss. Adjust seasonings.

Arugula Salad with Pears

Make a quick dressing with about ¼ cup olive oil, 2 tablespoons or so of fresh lemon juice, a teaspoon of honey, some salt and pepper and a bit of chopped fresh herb if you have any handy.

In a large salad bowl put the arugula, some crumbled goat cheese, a few chopped nuts, and two thinly sliced pears (peeled and cored). Toss with the dressing and enjoy!

Bok Choy

Whatever you call it – pak choi, pe-tsai, petsay, bac choi, white celery mustard or Chinese white cabbage – bok choy is a really healthy veggie. Being in a dieting frame of mind, I was thrilled to learn that bok choy is a negative-calorie food – the more you eat, the more calories you burn. Can't beat that with a stick. But it also has loads of great antioxidants, minerals, vitamins and dietary fiber. (For the full scoop: www.nutrition-and-you.com/bok-choy.html.) But it's also really delicious. Here are some quick and easy recipes for this great veggie, which works in any stir-fry.

Easiest Stove-top Bok Choy (amounts approximate)

A drizzle of olive oil
2 cloves garlic, minced
1 T. minced fresh ginger
Maybe 6-8 cups chopped bok choy
A couple tablespoons of soy sauce or Bragg's
Salt and pepper

Heat oil in a large skillet over medium heat, then add the garlic and ginger and cook for a minute. Add bok choy and soy sauce cook 3 to 5 minutes, until greens are wilted and stalks are crisp-tender. Season, to taste, with salt and black pepper. If you want a little extra flavor, toss in a spoon of toasted sesame seeds. Now, how easy was that?

Simplest Bok Choy Soup

6 - 8 cups of chicken or vegetable broth
A good tablespoon of minced fresh ginger
1 T. soy sauce or Bragg's (or to taste)
1 T. sesame oil
A generous pinch of crushed red pepper flakes
A clove or two of garlic
Some fresh mushrooms, sliced (optional)
About 3 cups bok choy cut in ribbons
A couple of green onions, sliced

Bring the broth to boil in a saucepan and stir in everything except for the bok choy and green onions. Simmer for 3 or 4 minutes, then add the bok choy and simmer until it is tender. Ladle into bowls and top with sliced green onion.

Note: You can ad lib on this just fine – leftover chicken bits or a few shrimp? Toss them in. Same for fresh grated carrots or even some broccoli florets. If you want to bulk it up, add some cellophane noodles at the start of cooking.

Bok Choy with Ginger

6-8 cups bok choy
About 1 T. vegetable oil
2 cloves garlic, finely minced
2-3 tsp. grated fresh ginger
2 T. low-sodium soy sauce
A splash of white wine or water
Salt to taste
½ tsp. sesame oil

Wash bok choy and trim just the very end part of the stem. Finely mince garlic and grate the fresh ginger.

Put your wok or frying pan on the stove, add the vegetable oil, garlic and ginger, and turn the heat to medium-high. Let the ginger and garlic gently sizzle in the oil. When they get fragrant and lightly brown, add the bok choy, and toss well to coat the leaves with this highly flavored oil. Add in the soy sauce and water or wine, cover and cook for about a minute. Season with salt and drizzle a little sesame oil on top.

Bok Choy Salad

In a small jar mix ½ cup olive oil, ¼ cup mild vinegar, 1/3 cup sugar and 3 T. soy sauce or Bragg's, and shake well.

In a salad bowl: Toss together bok choy (sliced into ribbons), some chopped green onions, a good handful of toasted almonds (chopped or slivered), and some dried cranberries for good measure. If you like those little crispy chow mein noodles, they add a nice crunch, too. Toss with your dressing and enjoy a delightful change from the standard dinner salad.

Stir-Fried Shanghai Bok Choy with Ginger

1 (2-inch) piece ginger, peeled
¾ lb. bok choy
¼ cup chicken broth
1 tsp. Chinese rice wine or Sherry
1 tsp. soy sauce
½ tsp. cornstarch
½ tsp. salt
¼ tsp. sugar
1 T. vegetable oil
½ tsp. sesame oil

Cut half the ginger into very fine matchsticks (less than 1/8 inch thick; about 1 tablespoon) and reserve. Finely grate remaining ginger. Trim 1/8-inch from bottom of bok choy, rinse and spin to dry leaves.

Whisk together ginger, chicken broth, rice wine, soy sauce, cornstarch, salt, and sugar in a small bowl until cornstarch is dissolved.
Heat wok over high heat until a bead of water vaporizes. Pour oil down side of wok, then swirl oil, tilting wok to coat sides. Add ginger matchsticks and stir-fry 5 seconds. Add bok choy and stir-fry until leaves are bright green and just limp, 1 to 2 minutes. Stir broth mixture, then pour into wok and stir-fry until vegetables are crisp-tender and sauce is slightly thickened, about 1 minute. Remove from heat and drizzle with sesame oil, then stir to coat.

Bok Choy with Lime Dressing

2 T. oil
3 red chiles cut into thin strips
3 garlic cloves thinly sliced
6 green onions sliced diagonally
2 head of bok choy sliced thin
1 T. crushed peanuts

Dressing:
2 T. lime juice
1-2 T. fish sauce
½ - 1 cup coconut milk

Dressing: Put the lime juice and fish sauce in a bowl and gradually whisk in the coconut milk until combined.

Heat the oil in a wok or skillet and stir-fry the chilies for 2-3 minutes or until crisp. Remove from pan. Add the garlic to the wok and stir-fry for 30-60 seconds or until golden. Remove from pan. Add scallions to the wok and stir-fry 2-3 minutes.

Bring a large pan of lightly salted water to a boil. Add the bok choy. Stir twice and then drain immediately. Mix the bok choy, garlic, chilies and scallions in a large serving bowl. Toss with dressing and garnish with crushed peanuts.

Goshen-style Spicy Indian Greens and Potatoes

½ tsp. cumin seeds
½ tsp. mustard seeds
2 tsp. cardamom pods
½ tsp. coriander seeds
¼ tsp. crushed red pepper

About 2 pounds of potatoes, boiled in the skin, cooled and cut into large dice
1 big clove garlic, minced
1 medium or ½ large onion, chopped
Several cups of assorted greens – tatsoi, arugula, bok choy etc. – rinsed and
   stemmed

Put the first five ingredients in a small skillet and toast lightly over medium
heat for a few minutes. When the mustard seeds start popping, remove from
heat. Throw the spices into your coffee grinder (wipe it out before – and
after!) and grind the toasted seeds into a powder. You will have more than
you need, but you can store the rest for later use; quite a lot of flavor and
heat.

In a large skillet, pour in a good drizzle of olive oil, then add the garlic and
onion and sauté for a couple of minutes. Add in a generous teaspoon or more
of your spice mixture and stir, then add in the potatoes and stir, making sure
that the potatoes are well coated with seasoning. Cook, stirring occasionally,
until potatoes start to brown up a little. Lastly, add the greens, stirring and
mixing well to coat leaves. Once greens have wilted – just a minute or two –
taste and adjust for seasoning, then serve.

Cabbage

Stuffed Cabbage Leaves

1 good-sized head cabbage
1 large onion, finely chopped
2 T. olive oil
½ lb. ground beef
½ lb. ground pork
1-½ cups cooked rice
2-3 cloves finely chopped garlic
A handful of chopped parsley (about ½ cup)
1 tsp. salt
¼ tsp. black pepper
About ½ cup fresh lemon juice
2 T. tomato paste
Broth, any type (see note below)
One lemon, sliced

Heat oven to 350 degrees. Carefully remove core from cabbage with a paring knife. Place whole head in a large pot filled with boiling, salted water, cover and cook 3 or 4 minutes, or until softened enough to pull off individual leaves. You'll need about 18 leaves.

When cool enough to handle, put a leaf with rib side up and trim down the thick center stem without cutting through the leaf – leaving it "flat" and easier to roll up. Repeat, then chop any leftover cabbage and place in the bottom of a Dutch oven or large covered casserole.

Sauté the chopped onion in olive oil until tender, and let it cool. Then mix the cooled onions with the beef, pork, rice, garlic, parsley, and salt and pepper until just combined.

Place about 1/3 cup of meat/rice mixture on each cabbage leaf. Roll away from you to encase the meat. Flip the right side of the leaf to the middle, then flip the left side. You will have something that looks like an envelope. Once again, roll away from you to create a neat little roll.

Place the cabbage rolls on top of the chopped cabbage in the Dutch oven, seasoning each layer with salt and pepper. Mix together the lemon juice, tomato paste and enough broth to make one cup, and pour over the rolls. Cover with lemon slices, then cover pot and bake for 1 hour or until cabbage is tender and meat is cooked. Serve with pan juices.

Cabbage and Radish Slaw with Asian Dressing

About 1 T. chopped fresh ginger
2 cloves of garlic, minced
A good ¼ cup of creamy peanut butter
Maybe ½ cup rice wine vinegar
3 T. soy sauce or Bragg's
3 T. brown sugar
¼ cup salad oil
1 small green cabbage, finely shredded
About 20 red radishes, cut into matchsticks
4 green onions, cut on the diagonal into long, thin slices
About ½ cup roasted peanuts

Blend ginger, garlic, peanut butter, vinegar, soy sauce, sugar and oil in a blender until smooth; set aside. Put cabbage, radishes, green onions and peanuts in a large serving bowl. Pour in peanut dressing; toss thoroughly to combine.

Chard

Connie's Favorite Chard

1 bunch chard, stems and center ribs cut out and chopped together, leaves
   coarsely chopped separately
3 slices bacon
1-2 cloves garlic, minced
½ small onion, diced
½ cup dry white wine
1 T. fresh lemon juice, or to taste
Small handful of cranberries
2 T. freshly grated Parmesan cheese
Salt to taste

In a pot, cook the bacon till crisp; remove and blot. Drain off most of the drippings, but leave about a tablespoon in the pot. Stir in the garlic and onion, and cook for 30 seconds until fragrant. Add the chard stems, cranberries and the white wine. Simmer until the stems begin to soften, about 5 minutes. Stir in the chard leaves, and cook until wilted – it will take just a minute. Finally, stir in lemon juice and Parmesan; season with salt as needed.

Garlicky Chard with Pine Nuts and Olives

A good bunch of chard
A handful of pine nuts (maybe ¼ cup)
Olive oil
Several garlic cloves, sliced
A good ¼ cup olives, pitted, chopped
Generous glug or two of red wine (or water, if you must)
Salt and pepper to taste

Separate stems and center ribs from chard, then chop leaves and stems separately. Toast the pine nuts in a large skillet over low heat, shaking the pan and stirring now and then, just until the nuts start to brown; remove and set aside. Add a little olive oil in the pan, then add the garlic and cook until it is soft and golden brown. Turn the heat to medium and add in the chard stems and olives, cook for a minute or two, then add the chard leaves, wine and a little S&P. Cook, stirring, until the leaves are wilted and most of the liquid has evaporated, then stir in the pine nuts and you're done! This is good hot or at room temperature.

Chard and Potato Pizza

Your favorite pizza dough (for a 12" pizza)
1 medium cooked potato, thinly sliced
6-8 leaves chard, stemmed and chopped
2 cloves garlic, minced
Olive oil
Generous sprinkle of paprika
2-3 ounces of cheese (combination of mozzarella and Parmesan is nice)

Preheat the oven to 425; if you have a pizza stone, put it in the oven while it is heating up. Heat a little oil in a skillet, add the garlic and chard, and sauté until the chard is wilted. Shape the crust on a baking sheet sprinkled with cornmeal, brush with a little olive oil. Top with the chard mixture and potato slices, sprinkle with a little more salt and the paprika, then scatter the cheese on top. Slide the pizza onto the pizza stone (or just put the baking sheet in the oven) and bake for maybe 10-12 minutes, or until the crust is nicely browned.

Baked Eggs on a Bed of Greens

One of my favorite meals, and so easy. You can even include a layer of grain — quinoa or rice — as a foundation, and get an even heartier meal.

4 eggs
About a pound of chard or spinach, slightly less of kale
1 T. butter
1 T. flour
A scant cup of milk
Salt and pepper
Pinch of nutmeg
About ½ cup grated Parmesan or other flavorful cheese

In a saucepan add about a half-inch of water, bring to a boil and add in your washed and chopped greens; cover and steam until greens are wilted. If using chard, chop stems and add them to the pot first to cook and soften. Remove greens from heat and drain.

In the same saucepan, melt the butter over medium-low heat, add the flour and stir into a thick paste. With a whisk, gradually add in milk and stir constantly until mixture thickens. Remove from heat, season with salt, pepper and nutmeg, and add half the cheese and your well-drained greens. Mix well. Pour greens mixture into a greased 8-inch casserole. With the back of a spoon, make four wells, crack an egg into each, season lightly with S&P and sprinkle with the rest of the cheese. Bake in a 400 oven for about 20 minutes, or until egg whites are set. Soooo good.

Chard and Feta Quiche

9-inch pie crust (your own or store bought; whole wheat crust with herbs is
    awesome)
2 tsp. extra-virgin olive oil
6 cups chopped chard, (about 1 bunch), leaves and stems separated
2 T. minced garlic
2 T. water
4 eggs
1 cup ricotta cheese
1 tsp. freshly grated lemon zest
1/8 tsp. freshly ground pepper
½ cup chopped pitted kalamata olives
1/3 cup crumbled feta cheese

Preheat oven to 400°F. Prepare your pie crust, roll out and fit into the pan; prick the bottom and sides with a fork in a few places. Bake until lightly brown – maybe 15 minutes. Cool on a rack for about 10 minutes.

While crust is baking, work on the filling. Heat oil in a large skillet over medium heat, add chard stems and cook until just tender, then add the garlic and stir briefly. Now add in the chard leaves and 2 T. water, stirring, until the leaves are just tender. Strain the greens and let drain and cool for 5 minutes or so. In a bowl whisk the eggs, ricotta, lemon zest and pepper. Fold in the greens, olives and feta, and pour the mixture into the crust. Bake until the top is lightly browned and a knife inserted in the center comes out clean, about a half-hour. Cool for a few minutes before serving. You can also eat this at room temperature.

Garlic scapes

Beautiful, curly and ephemeral – get them while you can!

White Bean and Garlic Scape Dip

3 or 4 garlic scapes, chopped
1 T. fresh lemon juice, more to taste
½ tsp. Kosher salt, or to taste
Ground black pepper to taste
1 can (15 ounces) cannellini beans, rinsed and drained
¼ cup extra virgin olive oil, more for drizzling.

In a food processor, process garlic scapes with lemon juice, salt and pepper until finely chopped. Add cannellini beans and process to a rough purée. With motor running, slowly drizzle olive oil through feed tube and process until fairly smooth. Pulse in 2 or 3 tablespoons water, or more, until mixture is the consistency of a dip. Add more salt, pepper and/or lemon juice, if desired. Spread out dip on a plate, drizzle with olive oil, and sprinkle with more salt. Serve with bread, tortilla chips, etc. Mmmm. I'm hungry.

Garlic Scape and Almond Pesto

10 garlic scapes, finely chopped
About ½ cup Parmesan cheese
1/3 cup chopped almonds (you could toast them lightly, if you'd like)
About ½ cup olive oil
Sea salt

Put the scapes, cheese, almonds and half the olive oil in a food processor (or use a blender). Whir to chop and blend all the ingredients and then add the remainder of the oil and, if you want, more cheese. If you like the texture, stop; if you'd like it a little thinner, add some more oil. Season with salt. By the way, you can freeze this for later in the summer.

Pasta Carbonara with Garlic Scapes and Chard
Serves 4

½ lb. pasta
4 slices bacon, chopped
¼ cup garlic scapes, cut into ¼ inch coins
1 bunch chard
2 large eggs
¼ tsp. kosher salt
¼ tsp. red pepper flakes
2 T. chopped fresh parsley
½ cup freshly grated Romano or Parmesan cheese

Set a pot of water to boiling and cook pasta til al dente. Meanwhile, cook the bacon over medium heat until browned. Remove the bacon pieces with a slotted spoon, drain off all but 1 T. of bacon fat, then add the garlic scapes and chard, cooking a couple of minutes until soft. Remove from the pan with a slotted spoon.

Whisk together the eggs, salt, parsley and red pepper flakes.

When the pasta is done, remove it from the stove, drain, and return to the pot. Put the pot back on low heat, stir in bacon, chard and scapes, then add the egg mixture and stir energetically for a couple of minutes until sauce is thick and creamy. Don't let it overcook or it will be gloppy. Sprinkle the grated cheese in a little at a time and stir to combine.

Frittata with Chard, Scapes and Parsley
Serves 6

1 bunch chard
¼ cup garlic scapes, cut into coins
1 cup chopped onion
Splash of olive oil
6 eggs
3 T. chopped fresh parsley
¼ tsp. salt
¼ tsp. black pepper

Chop the chard. In a skillet, sauté the scapes and onions in a little olive oil for about two minutes. Add the chard, cover and lower the heat; cook for a few minutes until the chard is wilted. Remove from heat and drain if it is too "juicy."

In a large bowl, beat the eggs, parsley, salt and pepper until blended. Stir in the chard mixture.

Heat a skillet on medium heat; once hot, add a shimmer of oil, then pour in the egg mixture. Cover and cook until the edges are firm and bottom is beginning to brown. Fun part – flip the frittata over (I do a skillet-to-plate-to-skillet transfer) and cover another 4-5 minutes until the eggs are cooked. You can either eat this right away or at room temperature.

Radishes

Roasted Radishes

Radishes
Extra-virgin olive oil
Kosher salt and freshly ground pepper
Fresh lemon juice

Toss radishes with oil. Season with salt and pepper. Roast on a baking sheet at 450 degrees, stirring once, until slightly tender and charred, about 15 minutes. Sprinkle with salt. Drizzle with lemon juice. Simple, good and different.

Bon Appetit's Raw Radishes and Greens

Radishes: Pile 16 – 20 scrubbed radishes with their green leaves still attached onto a plate. Set out a bowl of coarse sea salt and a dish of slightly softened butter. Pick up a radish, spread a bit of butter on it, sprinkle with salt, and eat!

Greens: Place radish leaves in a bowl. Drizzle the leaves with Dijon Vinaigrette, season to taste with S&P and enjoy as a salad.

Dijon Vinaigrette

1 T. fresh lemon juice
1 tsp. Dijon mustard
1 T. white wine vinegar
1 garlic clove, finely minced
½ cup extra virgin olive oil
Salt and freshly ground black pepper

Whisk lemon juice, mustard, vinegar and garlic in a bowl. Gradually whisk in oil, season to taste with salt and pepper. Can be saved in fridge for three days, but bring to room temperature before using.

Tatsoi

OK, honestly. Who grew up with tatsoi? What a shame – think of all we missed! It is a nice, versatile green – you can mix it with other lettuces in a salad, add it at the last minute to stir-fries, add into soups, sauté just like any other green. In other words, be inventive.

Chilled Wilted Tatsoi Salad with Sesame-Ginger Dressing

10-12 ounces Tatsoi leaves
Sesame seeds, for garnish

Dressing:
2 T. soy sauce
1 T. rice vinegar
1 tsp. grated ginger root
1 tsp. sugar
½ tsp. Sriracha (or other type of Asian hot chile sauce)
Fresh ground black pepper to taste

Bring a pot of salted water to a boil, and fill another bowl with cold water and a handful of ice cubes. Wash tatsoi leaves and cut into thick strips. Dump tatsoi into boiling water, time for exactly one minute, then drain immediately into colander and dump into bowl with ice water.

While tatsoi is cooling in ice water, get a plastic bowl with a tight fitting lid that's large enough to hold all the tatsoi. Mix dressing ingredients in this bowl, then drain tatsoi well and add to dressing. Chill in the refrigerator an hour or more, turning bowl over a few times so tatsoi remains coated with the dressing. To serve, use tongs or a slotted spoon to remove tatsoi from bowl and arrange on serving plates. Toast sesame seeds for 1-2 minutes in a dry pan and sprinkle over salad.

Peanut Egg Noodle Tatsoi – from *SparkRecipes*
Serves 4

6 cups tatsoi (or bok choy or spinach), chopped
1 ½ cups raw carrots, chopped
3 cloves garlic
2 T. olive oil
1 tsp. sesame oil
¼ cup chopped onion
¼ cup chopped onion
3 ½ cups cooked egg noodles

Sauce:
5 T. natural peanut butter
1 T. white wine vinegar
3 T. soy or tamari sauce
1 T. olive oil

Cook noodles according to directions; drain. Sauté oil and garlic 5 minutes. Add carrots and onion and sauté 5 minutes. Add tatsoi; sauté till tender. Mix together ingredients for sauce. Pour over vegetable mixture. Stir-fry a few minutes. Serve over egg noodles.

Basic Stir-Fried Greens with Shrimp

Everybody has their own way of doing stir-fry; this is mine, and it's pretty basic. You can add in just about any kind of vegetable you want, as long as you follow a few simple rules: 1) Chop everything before you start cooking; 2) Keep the heat high to cook the food quickly and keep it from getting soggy; and 3) Cook the tenderest vegetables last. It's not necessary to use a wok. I don't have one anymore so I just use a large pot. By the way, this is still good without the shrimp, so works well as a vegetarian dish, too. This recipe should give you about four good servings.

1-2 T. vegetable oil
2-3 cloves garlic, minced
A chunk of fresh ginger, peeled and diced (~ 2 T)
A fresh hot chili, seeded and minced
½ pound raw shrimp, peeled
Handful of peanuts
2 carrots, peeled and sliced on the diagonal
2 stalks celery, sliced on the diagonal
4-5 green onions, chopped (green and white parts)
About 1 ½ pounds of tatsoi &/or bok choy (maybe 4-5 BIG handfuls); chop
    large stems to 1 inch
1-2 tsp. sesame oil
1 tsp. sesame seeds
3-4 T. soy sauce or Bragg's
About ½ cup chicken or veg broth mixed with
1 tsp. cornstarch

Heat your wok or pot on high heat, then add oil. When it shimmers, add garlic, ginger and chili and stir for about a minute. Add shrimp and peanuts, stirring and tossing gently until shrimp are pink, about 3-4 minutes. Remove with slotted spoon and reserve.

If necessary, add another little drizzle of oil to your pot, then add carrots, celery and green onions. Cook, stirring, for 3-4 minutes, add the greens and stir until these begin to wilt. Add the sesame oil and seeds, soy sauce and broth mixed with cornstarch, and add the shrimp back in. Stir the mixture well, stirring until the sauce thickens. Taste and adjust seasonings, and serve over rice or noodles.

Browned Butter Pasta with Tatsoi – adapted from Backyard Farming

Your pasta of choice, preferably curved or with ridges
½ stick unsalted butter
Salt and pepper
About 3-4 cups tatsoi, rinsed
½ cup fresh sage leaves
Freshly grated Parmesan
Lemon wedges, optional

Cook pasta to al dente in salted water; drain well. As pasta is cooking, melt butter in a skillet. Swirl the butter in the pan as it foams. When butter begins to brown, toss in sage leaves and cook until leaves are crisp and brown; remove with a slotted spoon and throw away. Add in drained pasta and mix to coat with browned butter. Salt and pepper to taste. Add tatsoi and cook until slightly wilted, about 1 to 2 minutes. Plate and serve immediately with grated Parmesan and lemon wedges on the side.

Gingery Sautéed Tatsoi with Tofu Steaks – from *Food Blogga*
Serves 2

2 T. soy sauce
¼ tsp. rice vinegar
2 tsp. brown sugar
2 tsp. lime juice
2 tsp. minced fresh ginger
¼ tsp. cayenne pepper
6 oz. extra firm tofu, cut into "steaks"
1 T. sesame oil, divided
2 small bunches of tatsoi (2-3 cups)
1-2 tsp. toasted sesame seeds

In a small bowl whisk all ingredients from soy sauce through cayenne pepper.

In a large skillet over medium high heat, add 2 teaspoons sesame oil. Add tofu steaks; cook for 5-7 minutes per side, or until golden brown. Remove from skillet. Add remaining 1 teaspoon sesame oil to skillet; add tatsoi; once wilted, add sauce. Reduce heat to medium-low, and cook just until sauce slightly thickens. Divide greens on plates. Top with half of the tofu. Drizzle with remaining sauce, and sprinkle with sesame seeds. Serve immediately.

Turnip Greens

Here are some recipes for turnip greens — an early-in-the-season treat that you might otherwise decide to put in the compost pile. They are also incredibly nutritious. According to The World's Healthiest Foods (www.whfoods.com), turnip greens are an excellent source of many vitamins including vitamin K, vitamin A (in the form of beta-carotene), vitamin C, vitamin E, vitamin B6, folate, manganese, fiber, calcium, and copper. In addition, they are a very good source of potassium, magnesium, iron, vitamin B2, phosphorus, vitamin B1, vitamin B3, vitamin B5, omega-3 fatty acids, and protein. So what are you waiting for?

Sautéed Fresh Turnip Greens
Serves 4

1 lb. fresh turnip greens
1 tsp. salt
1 hard cooked egg
1/3 cup minced green pepper
2 tsp. fresh lemon juice
1/3 cup chopped onion
1/2 tsp. sugar
2 strips bacon
¼ tsp. black pepper

Wash turnip greens thoroughly. Trim off coarse stems. Fry bacon until crisp and remove it from the fat. Add onion and green pepper to bacon fat and sauté until limp. Coarsely chop turnip greens and add to onions and green pepper. Stir to mix well. Cover tightly and cook 10 - 15 minutes, or until tender. Add salt, black pepper, sugar and lemon juice. Toss lightly. Turn into serving dish and garnish with crisp, crumbled bacon and slices of hard cooked egg.

Meatless Turnip Greens with a Kick

1 T. olive oil
1 shallot, chopped
1 clove garlic, chopped
1 tsp. red pepper flakes
1 ½ lbs. turnip greens, washed, stemmed and chopped
Freshly ground black pepper
2 T. Dijon mustard
1 cup vegetable stock
½ cup chopped pecans, toasted

Heat olive oil in Dutch oven over medium heat. Add shallot, garlic and red pepper flakes and sauté until tender and fragrant. Add the washed and cleaned turnip greens. Mix together. Cook until they have wilted down, about 3 minutes. Add pepper to taste.

In a small bowl, whisk the Dijon mustard with the chicken stock. Add to the wilted greens and cook until the liquid has all but evaporated. Add the toasted pecans and serve immediately.

Hot Wilted Greens
Serves 4

1 thick slice smoky bacon
2 tsp. olive oil
1 large clove garlic, minced
1 medium sweet red onion
3 T. chicken stock
2 T. balsamic vinegar
1 quart mixed piquant leafy greens (such as arugula, turnip greens, endive or
    mustard greens)
¼ cup toasted pecans

In a large, deep skillet or wok over medium heat, cook bacon until crispy. Remove and drain on paper towels. Crumble and reserve. Add olive oil to bacon drippings in skillet, heat and add garlic and onions. Sauté for 3-4 minutes, until onions and garlic are softened. Stir in chicken stock and vinegar. Add greens and mix. Stir-fry for 2-3 minutes, until leaves are coated. Cover and cook several minutes more, until leaves are wilted and cooked tender-crisp. Top with bacon and chopped pecans. Serve hot.

Mess o' Greens Salad With Warm Pecan Dressing

6 cups fresh turnip or mustard greens, collards or arugula (about 1 pound)
2 T. balsamic vinegar
2 tsp. honey
1 T. Dijon mustard
2 tsp. vegetable oil
½ cup pecans, roughly chopped or broken

Wash greens well, dry thoroughly, then remove and discard the long stems.
Tear the greens into salad-size pieces and place in a large bowl.

In a small bowl, combine the vinegar, honey and mustard. Set aside.

Heat the oil in a small skillet until hot but not smoking. Add the vinegar
mixture and pecans and cook, stirring regularly, for 2 to 3 minutes. Pour over
the greens and serve at once.

Chapter 2

A hint of summer: Early-days vegetables

The garden is getting exciting now, with a whole new crop of substantial vegetables that herald the start of summer – lovely summer squashes and cucumbers (prickly to harvest), fresh basil and rosemary. And let's not forget kale, that miracle of nutrition, taste and versatility.

Basil

Classic Basil Pesto

2 cups packed fresh basil leaves
2 cloves garlic
¼ cup pine nuts
2/3 cup extra-virgin olive oil, divided
Salt and freshly ground black pepper, to taste
½ cup freshly grated Pecorino or Parmesan cheese

Combine the basil, garlic and pine nuts in a food processor and pulse until coarsely chopped. Add ½ of the oil and process until fully incorporated and smooth. Season with salt and pepper. Add the remaining oil and pulse until smooth, finally adding in the cheese and stirring to mix.

Beets

Roasted Beet Salad

One bunch of beets
¼ cup water

3 T. balsamic vinegar
1 T. honey
1½ tsp. red wine vinegar
¼ tsp. ground black pepper
¼ cup chopped sweet onion

¼ cup chopped walnuts
1/3 cup crumbled blue cheese
A little chopped fresh parsley
Salt to taste

Preheat oven to 400 degrees. Arrange beets in a baking dish and pour in water; cover with aluminum foil. Bake until beets are tender, about 1 hour. Allow beets to cool, remove outer skin and chop into bite-size pieces.

Whisk the vinegar, honey, red wine vinegar and pepper together in a salad bowl. Stir beets, onion and walnuts into vinegar dressing. Sprinkle with blue cheese, parsley and salt to serve.

Beets Caramelized in Honey, Soy and Walnuts

8 medium beets, washed
1½ cups soy sauce
3 T. honey
1 2-inch piece ginger, grated
2 T. olive oil
1¾ oz. raw walnuts
3 T. brown sugar
Sea salt and freshly ground black pepper, to taste

Preheat oven to 350 F. Arrange the beets on a baking tray and toss with the soy sauce, honey, ginger and olive oil until evenly coated. Sprinkle with the walnuts and brown sugar and season to taste. Roast for 40 minutes to an hour, or until sticky and caramelized.

Halve the tender beets and serve warm, drizzled with the pan juices, as part of a salad or to accompany a meat dish.

Cucumber

Cold Cucumber Soup

Olive oil
1 large onion, diced
1 or 2 cloves of garlic
2 large cucumbers, peeled and diced
1 large potato, peeled and diced
4 cups broth – chicken or vegetable
Parsley, salt and pepper
A little bit of half and half, milk or soy/rice milk (unsweetened)

In a large deep skillet or soup pot, sauté the onion and garlic until the onion is transparent. Add the chopped cukes and cook, stirring, for a couple of minutes. Add the broth and potatoes, bring to a boil, then reduce heat, allowing soup to simmer for 10 minutes. Remove from heat and allow to cool. Thoroughly blend in batches, seasoning with parsley, salt and pepper to taste. Put blended mixture in refrigerator and allow to chill thoroughly. Before serving, stir in a little of the light cream or milk, and adjusting seasonings to taste. (It looks really pretty served with a ribbon of cucumber and small dollop of sour cream as garnish.)

Basic Andaluz Gazpacho

There is an actual recipe below, but really, you can ad lib with gazpacho depending on what you've got on hand. A simple rule of thumb is three parts tomatoes to one part other ingredients – red, yellow or green bell peppers, onions, garlic, scallions, peeled cucumbers – all cut into chunks.

Pack the vegetables in the blender, starting with the tomatoes because they're the juiciest. Add a decent splash of red wine vinegar or sherry vinegar and a bigger splash of olive oil and season with salt and freshly ground pepper, then puree until chunky or smooth. If you want to make a thicker gazpacho, soak a few pieces of country bread in water, squeeze dry and add them to the blender along with the vegetables.

Test for seasoning, adding salt & pepper, and more vinegar or oil, as needed, and refrigerate several hours or overnight. Serve it on its own or garnished with finely diced vegetables, crisp croutons, diced avocado – even shrimp or lobster. Have fun, and don't forget to have a nice bottle of Spanish wine on hand.

3 lbs. ripe tomatoes, peeled, seeded and chopped (about 6 cups)
1 cup chopped onion
1 large sweet pepper (any color), seeded and chopped
1 T. chopped garlic
2 tsp. chopped, seeded jalapeno, or to taste
1 ½ cups peeled and cubed cucumbers
1-2 pieces crusty bread, soaked in water and squeezed fairly dry (optional)
4-5 T. fresh herb (cilantro, dill, parsley or basil all work); coarsely chop
¼ cup olive oil
3 T. red wine vinegar
Salt and freshly ground black pepper to taste

Combine all ingredients in the food processor or blender and puree until either chunky or smooth, as you wish. Taste and adjust seasonings, transfer to a pitcher, and chill, covered, in the refrigerator until it is nice and cold. Serve with crusty bread.

Kale

Kale, Apple and Pancetta Salad
Serves 6

1/3 cup olive oil
4 oz. pancetta, diced
¼ cup white wine vinegar
¼ cup pure maple syrup
¼ tsp. salt
¼ tsp. freshly ground black pepper
1 small head radicchio, shredded
½ lb. kale, stems discarded, leaves shredded
2 tart yet sweet apples, sliced into thick matchsticks
¾ cup pecans (toasted is even better)

Combine the olive oil and pancetta in a small saucepan over medium heat.
Cook, stirring frequently, until pancetta is golden and crispy. Strain the pan
drippings into a small bowl and leave the crispy pancetta off to the side to
cool. To the oil add the vinegar, maple syrup, salt and pepper and whisk well.

Combine the radicchio, kale, apples and pecans in a large bowl. Toss while
adding the dressing, little by little, until salad is well dressed. Taste and adjust
seasoning with salt and pepper. Garnish with crispy pancetta.

Kale-Apple Smoothie
One serving

¾ cup chopped kale, ribs and thick stems removed
1 small stalk celery, chopped
½ banana
½ cup apple juice
½ cup ice
1 T. fresh lemon juice

Place all the ingredients in a blender, then blend until smooth and frothy.

Super Energy Kale Soup
Serves 4

1 medium onion, chopped
4 cloves garlic, chopped
1 T. olive oil
5 cups chicken or vegetable broth
1 cup ¼-inch dice carrot
½ cup diced celery
2 red potatoes in ½-inch dice
3 cups kale, stems removed and leaves chopped fine
2 tsp. dried thyme
2 tsp. dried sage
Salt and pepper to taste

Chop garlic and onions. Heat a tablespoon of olive oil in a medium soup pot, sauté the onion for 3-4 minutes, then add garlic and sauté for another minute or so. Add broth, carrots and celery and bring to a boil on high heat. Once boiling, reduce heat to a simmer and continue to cook for another 5 minutes. Add potatoes and cook until tender, about 15 more minutes. Add kale and seasonings and cook another 5 minutes.

White Bean and Sausage Ragout with Tomatoes, Kale and Zucchini
4 servings

1 T. olive oil
½ cup chopped onion
½ lb. sausage links (any kind), cut into ½-inch slices
1 zucchini, quartered and cut into ½ -inch slices (about 2 cups)
3 garlic cloves, peeled and crushed
6 cups chopped trimmed kale (about 1/2 pound)
½ cup water
2 16-oz. cans cannellini beans or other white beans, rinsed and drained
1 lb. diced tomatoes (if using canned, do not drain)
Salt and pepper to taste

Heat oil in a large skillet over medium-high heat. Sauté onion and sausage 4 minutes or until sausage is browned. Add zucchini and garlic; cook 2 minutes. Add kale and remaining ingredients; bring to a boil. Cover, reduce heat, and simmer 10 minutes or until thoroughly heated. Serve immediately.

Kale and White Bean Soup
Serves 8

2 T. olive oil
4 cloves garlic, chopped
2 stalks celery, slices
1 large onion, chopped
1 ½ tsp. salt
½ tsp. pepper
2 15.5-oz. cans cannellini beans, rinsed
1 cup small soup pasta, such as orzo or tubettini (4 oz.)
1 bunch kale (8 cups), thick stems discarded and leaves torn in 2-inch pieces
2 T. chopped fresh rosemary
½ cup shaved Parmesan
1 T. fresh lemon juice

Heat the oil in a large pot over medium-high heat. Add the garlic, celery, onion, salt and pepper and cook, stirring occasionally, until tender, 4 to 6 minutes. Add the beans, pasta, kale, rosemary and 8 cups water, cover and bring to a boil. Reduce heat and simmer until the pasta and kale are tender, 4 to 5 minutes. Stir in the lemon juice and sprinkle with the shaved Parmesan before serving.

Kale Mallung (Sri Lankan Kale and Coconut)
Serves 4

1 medium red onion, chopped
1 to 2 hot chile peppers, seeded and chopped
12 oz. kale, stems removed and leaves thinly sliced
¼ tsp. ground cumin
Generous grating of black pepper
½ cup shredded coconut, fresh or frozen
1 to 2 T. lime juice
Salt to taste

Heat a large, deep skillet. Add the onions and peppers, and cook, stirring often, until onions soften and turn pink. Add water by the tablespoon if needed to prevent sticking.

Add the kale and a splash (about ¼ cup) of water, along with the cumin and pepper. Cover and cook, stirring every minute or so, until kale is wilted but still bright green, about 4 to 5 minutes. Add the coconut and 1 T. lime juice and leave on the heat just long enough to heat through. Check the seasoning and add more lime juice if needed and salt to taste. Serve hot or cold.

Kale too healthy for you? Make chips!

Even though kale is the most nutritious vegetable out there, it can be an acquired taste – especially if you didn't grow up eating greens. Try these fabulous kale chips – healthy but so good that your kids (and you) will eat them up like potato chips. I saw a tiny little package of them recently at the grocery store for $7.50 – so you can feel virtuous about saving money, too.

Kale Chips 1

1 large bunch kale, any variety
1 T. olive oil
Sea salt or Parmesan cheese

Preheat oven to 350°. Wash and spin kale leaves, pat dry. For curly kale, remove the stem and tear the leaves into bite-size pieces. For Tuscan or "dinosaur" kale, leave leaf whole. In a large bowl, toss gently with the olive oil and, if using, sprinkle with Parmesan, then spread in a single layer on a baking sheet. Bake 10-15 minutes, then gently turn over and return to oven until the kale is crispy and brown around the edges. Remove from oven. If you omitted the Parmesan, now is the time to sprinkle with sea salt. You can store these in an airtight container, but you probably won't have to.

Kale Chips 2

1 large bunch kale, any variety
1 T. olive oil
1-2 tsp. Bragg's liquid or soy sauce
2 T. nutritional yeast

Preheat oven to 350° and prepare kale as above. Mix together olive oil and Bragg's, pour over kale and toss gently. Spread in a single layer on baking sheet, sprinkle with the nutritional yeast and mix in a little, then bake as above. The Bragg's and the yeast can be pretty salty, so go easy the first time. Deliciously addictive!

Basic Big-Veggie Frittata with Greens

This is one of those use-what-you've got recipes, which makes it great for the CSA months and a fine way to use up veggie leftovers. With a grateful nod to Mark Bittman, this version of frittata relies more heavily on veggies and less on eggs. Don't think quiche – think a tasty wedge of vegetables bound together with a little egg. The rule of thumb: use one egg for every two cups of vegetables. Three eggs will make a generous frittata.

Olive oil
Half an onion, minced
1 fat clove garlic, minced
A couple of chopped garlic scapes, if you've got them
Salt and pepper
4-5 cups chopped greens – chard, spinach, kale or any combination
One medium cooked and cooled potato (use leftovers or microwave one)
A handful of chopped fresh herbs – basil, parsley, a little rosemary or mint
3 eggs
About ½ cup Parmesan or other hard cheese (optional)

Put a drizzle of olive oil in a large skillet over medium heat, add the onion, garlic and scapes, add in S&P and cook until soft, about 3 minutes. Add in the chopped greens and cook, stirring, until greens are wilted. (Note: If you are using chard, add in the chopped stems first and cook for a few minutes before adding in the leaves.) Add in the diced potato and the fresh herbs and cook for another few minutes.

In a small bowl, whisk the eggs with some salt and pepper and the cheese, then pour over the vegetables. Tilt the pan to distribute the egg as evenly as possible. Reduce the heat to low and cook for about 10 minutes, or until the egg is set. I like to cover the skillet for the last 4-5 minutes to help the egg set. Cut your frittata into wedges. You can serve this hot, warm or cold, so it makes a fabulous left-over for lunch the next day. You can also use zucchini, carrots, broccoli – any vegetable – as long as you cook them a little first and keep the proportion of one egg to two cups of veggies.

Summer Squash

Matchstick Summer Squash and Carrot Sauté

This lets you barely cook the veggies – just enough to take the rawness out of them but leave in all the flavor and goodness. I like to use both green and yellow squash for visual impact, but that's not essential.

A couple of zucchini or any kind of summer squash
A few carrots
A little olive oil
Couple cloves of garlic
A generous sprinkle of dried basil or a tablespoon of chopped fresh, plus salt and pepper

Wash and dry the squash, trim ends but do not peel! Wash and trim the carrots, peel if you want but it's not necessary. Cut the veggies into matchsticks. (I found a cheap little peeler gizmo at the grocery that juliennes veggies in a snap; it's just like peeling something but it scrapes out the little matchsticks.)

Heat a little olive oil in a skillet; add minced garlic and stir for a minute or two. Add in the carrots and stir for a minute, then add the squash. Stir frequently until vegetables have softened, maybe three or four minutes. Remove from heat, season with basil, S&P and serve.

Raw veggie salad #1

How great is this on a hot day? Cut the kernels off 3 ears of fresh raw corn and put in a bowl. Very thinly slice 2 medium (3 small) zucchini and add to the bowl. Drizzle about 2 tablespoons of good olive oil, 2 tablespoons of fresh lime juice, a good couple of tablespoons of chopped cilantro, salt and pepper, and stir well. Serve immediately (squash tends to get watery as it sits).

Raw veggie salad #2

Shred small zucchini and summer squash in a food processor or hand grater – you want them to be sort of match-stick size. Stir in some good Parmesan cheese, olive oil, salt and pepper, and bingo – another fresh salad to be eaten pronto.

Grilled Squash with Pesto

Slice unpeeled zucchini and/or yellow squash lengthwise (about ¼- ½ inch thick), brush with olive oil and cook on the grill, about 2-3 minutes a side, until they are nicely charred. Serve with a dollop of fresh pesto (recipe on page 32).

Easiest Stuffed Squash with Herbs and Goat Cheese

Two or three similarly sized summer squash (zucchini works great because of its round, even shape)
About ¼ cup of olive oil
A clove of garlic
2-3 T. of fresh herbs, minced (thyme, mint, chive, oregano, basil etc.)
About 2-3 oz. of goat cheese
Some plain breadcrumbs
A little bit of Parmesan cheese

Press a clove of garlic into the olive oil, stir it and let it sit while you prepare the squash. Cut the zucchini in half lengthwise. With a melon baller or a spoon, scoop out the fleshy, seedy center and create a well, taking care not to cut too close to the skin. Put the halves snugly into a baking dish. Put a drizzle of your garlicky olive oil into each squash half, season with salt and pepper, and put an equal amount of minced herbs into each half. Crumble the goat cheese and divide among the squash, then sprinkle a tablespoon or two of breadcrumbs on top. Use what's left of your garlic olive oil to drizzle over the top, sprinkle with a little Parmesan cheese and bake at 450 degrees for about 20-25 minutes.

Stuffed Pattypan Squash

This is pretty similar to the recipe above, but with pattypan squash, it's best to parboil the squash first for a few minutes to soften the outer skin.

6 small or 3-4 large pattypan squash
6 slices bacon
½ cup diced onion
1 cup soft bread crumbs
¼ cup freshly grated Parmesan cheese
Salt and pepper to taste

Preheat oven to 350. Bring one inch of water to a boil in a saucepan over medium-high heat. Add squash, cover and cook for 10 minutes, or until a fork can pierce the stem with little resistance. Drain and let it cool before trying to handle it. Slice off the top stem of the squash. Use a melon baller to carefully scoop out the centers of the squash, and reserve those bits for the next step.

Cook the bacon in a large skillet until evenly brown; remove to paper towels. Sauté the onion in bacon drippings, then add the chopped reserved squash pieces and sauté with the onion for a minute or so. Remove the skillet from heat, and stir in the breadcrumbs. Crumble in the bacon, and stir into the stuffing along with the Parmesan cheese. Season to taste with salt and pepper. Stuff each squash to overflowing with the mixture, and place them in a baking dish. Cover the dish loosely with aluminum foil. Bake for 15 minutes in the preheated oven, or until squash are heated through.

Zucchini "Crab" Cakes
Makes 8

2 ½ cups of zucchini, grated
1 cup of fine bread crumbs
1 egg, beaten
2 T. margarine, melted
1 generous tablespoon of Old Bay seasoning
4 T. of flour
1 small onion, chopped fine
Oil and margarine, for frying

Mix all ingredients together (except the oil/margarine) until well blended. Shape into patties – yields about 8. Fry over medium heat in a mixture of half oil/half margarine until golden on each side. Turn only once, and don't be hasty; you want these to cook through and get firm, not mushy. Drain on paper towels. Serve hot.

I made an instant sauce with mayo, Dijon mustard and dried dill – great on top. It would be perfect plated up on a bed of arugula or other spicy greens.

Zucchini chips

¼ cup dry breadcrumbs
¼ cup grated Parmesan cheese
¼ tsp. seasoned salt
¼ tsp. garlic powder
1/8 tsp. freshly ground black pepper
2 T. milk
2 ½ cups (¼-inch-thick) slices zucchini (about 2 small)
Cooking spray

Preheat oven to 425°. Combine the dry ingredients in a medium bowl, stirring with a whisk. Place milk in a shallow bowl. Dip zucchini slices in milk, and dredge in breadcrumb mixture. Place coated slices on an ovenproof wire rack coated with cooking spray; place rack on a baking sheet. Bake for 30 minutes or until browned and crisp. Serve immediately.

Refrigerator Bread and Butter Pickles (yields 4 cups)

About 1 ½ pounds small zucchini or cucumbers
1 ½ T. kosher salt
1 cup thinly sliced onion
1 cup white sugar
¼ cup packed light brown sugar
1 cup white vinegar
½ cup apple cider vinegar
1 ½ tsp. mustard seeds
½ tsp. celery seeds
1/8 tsp. ground turmeric

Wash zucchinis/cukes and trim the ends, but do not peel. Slice into ¼-inch rounds and combine with the salt in a bowl. Cover with a couple cups of ice cubes and leave in the fridge for an hour or so. Rinse in a colander to remove salt, drain well and return to the bowl.

In a medium saucepan, combine sugars, vinegars, seeds and turmeric. Bring to a simmer, stirring until sugar dissolves. Pour over cucumbers/zucchini and onions. Let sit at room temperature for an hour, then cover and refrigerate for 24 hours before serving. If you want, you can divide these into jars. The pickles have to stay refrigerated, but they will last for at least a couple of weeks (unless your family eats them all up sooner, which is highly likely).

Chapter 3

Some like it hot: Nightshades and more

Did you know that eggplant, tomatoes, potatoes and peppers of all varieties are part of the nightshade family? Nightshade is the common name to describe more than 2,800 species of plants – including the spooky, pharmaceutical ones like mandrake and belladonna (aka "deadly nightshade") – as well as tobacco. The good news is that your CSA nightshades are all highly edible and not a bit toxic. This is also the season for green and wax beans. And if you're lucky, your farmer also raises free-range chickens and laying hens – always in season.

Beans – Green and Wax

Wax or Green Beans with Honey, Lemon and a Kick

About 1 lb. of beans, ends trimmed
2 tsp. or so of honey
Grated zest from one lemon
A good pinch of cayenne (go easy or omit if you don't want the kick)
Salt to taste

Add beans to a pot of boiling water and cook until they are just tender –
maybe 6 or 7 minutes. Drain beans, then immediately toss with the honey,
zest, cayenne and salt. Try it. You'll like it!

Green Bean and Tomato Salad

Two or three big handfuls of green beans, stemmed
Two big tomatoes (or a few smaller ones)
A tablespoon or two of chopped fresh basil
1 tsp. fresh oregano
Several razor-thin slices of onion
A few swirls of olive oil and a light hand on the vinegar (to taste)
Salt and freshly ground pepper

Boil or steam the green beans until just tender; drain and plunge into cold
water. Drain again and chop into one-inch pieces. Dice the tomatoes (not
too small), cut several thin slices of onion and chop the fresh basil. Put all the
vegetables and herbs in a bowl, taking care to separate all the onion rings.
Add the oil, vinegar, S&P, mix well and chill in the fridge for an hour or so.

Sautéed Beans

1 lb. beans
2 cloves of garlic, finely minced
Olive oil
Salt & Pepper
Fresh herbs if you have any
About ¼ cup water

Wash and trim the beans; pat dry. Heat a large skillet to medium high, and when it's hot, add a tablespoon or two of olive oil. When the oil gets shimmery, add in the minced garlic, stir around, then add in the beans. Stir for a few minutes, add in the herbs and seasoning, then pour in just a small amount of water – about ¼ cup or less – and cover your skillet. Turn down the heat and let your beans finish cooking, about 5 minutes.

Roasted Beans with Three Variations

The basic recipe: Wash and trim a pound of beans; pat dry. Preheat the oven to 450 degrees. On a rimmed baking sheet, toss the beans with a tablespoon or so of olive oil, salt and pepper, and finely minced garlic or garlic powder. Roast until they get tender and brown in spots, about 15 minutes, but shake the pan halfway through. Eat them as is, or add one of the following variations:

Parmesan and lemon: When the beans come out of the oven, toss them with Parmesan cheese and grated lemon zest.

Asian style: While beans are roasting, combine about a tablespoon of soy sauce, a teaspoon of grated fresh ginger, maybe a teaspoon of lemon juice and a teaspoon of brown sugar. When beans are roasted, toss with this sauce, some chopped peanuts and a little cilantro.

With bacon or pancetta: Before roasting the beans, dice maybe 3-4 ounces of thick-slice bacon or pancetta and toss with the beans and other ingredients.

Eggplant
You are likely to come across the familiar fat aubergine eggplant, and the lesser-known but elegantly slender light purple Asian eggplant.

Easiest Asian Eggplant (my favorite)

Any number of Asian eggplant
Olive oil
Garlic
Maybe sprinkle of salt and pepper

Mince or press a clove or two of garlic into a small dish of olive oil (2-3 tablespoons), mix and set aside. Cut the stem end off the eggplant and cut in two, lengthwise. Do not peel.

Heat your grill (or grill pan, if you are an indoor-sy cook). Brush some of the garlicky olive oil onto both sides of your eggplant halves and start grilling. It doesn't take long for these tender eggplant to cook – maybe a few minutes on each side. They are delicious – creamy on the inside, and the skin gets a little crispy. Season with S&P if you think they need it. If you have little tiny ones, you can even grill them whole.

Grilled Eggplant and variations
I swear grilled eggplant is a different vegetable than the mushy, greasy fried thing served up in too many places.

2-3 small eggplant (or one large)
2-3 T. olive oil
2 T. balsamic vinegar
2 cloves garlic, minced
1 pinch each dried thyme, basil, dill and oregano
Salt and pepper
Squeeze of fresh lemon juice

Heat grill. When grill is hot, slice eggplant about 1/2-inch thick. (If you have the tiny little eggplants, you can just cut them in half or even do them whole; experiment.) Brush both sides of the eggplant slices with the oil and vinegar mixture.

Place eggplant on the hot preheated grill. Grill about 15 to 20 minutes, turning once. When they are done, squeeze a little lemon juice on them.

Variations: Instead of olive oil and balsamic vinegar, use soy sauce, grated ginger, sesame oil and a pinch of sugar. OR use sesame oil, curry powder and fresh chopped mint leaves

Eggplant Antipasto (make a day ahead)

This is luscious when you pair it with nice crusty bread, sliced thin and toasted. (A glass of wine goes nicely, too.)

1 large (or 2-3 small) eggplant, peeled, cubed
1 onion, chopped
2-3 cloves garlic, minced
1/3 cup chopped green pepper
About 1 cup sliced mushrooms
1/3 cup olive oil
¼ cup water
½ cup stuffed green olives, sliced
1 tsp. salt
1 6-oz. can tomato paste
2 T. red wine vinegar
1 ½ tsp. white sugar
¼ tsp. dried basil
¼ tsp. dried oregano

Preheat oven to 350 degrees. In a medium baking dish, mix the eggplant, onion, garlic, green pepper, mushrooms and olive oil. Cook covered 10 minutes in the preheated oven.

Remove the eggplant mixture from the oven and stir in the water, sliced stuffed green olives, salt, tomato paste, red wine vinegar, sugar, basil, oregano and pepper. Continue baking 30 minutes, or until the eggplant is tender.

Chill the mixture in the refrigerator 8 hours or overnight before serving.

Roasted Eggplant Soup
Serves 4-6

3 medium or 2 large eggplants, sliced in half lengthwise
Whole cumin seeds (or ground cumin)
Olive oil
1 ½ - 2 lbs. fresh tomatoes, diced
1 large onion, chopped
4-5 celery stalks, chopped
About a quart of chicken or vegetable stock
¼ cup parsley, finely chopped
2-3 garlic cloves, whole
¼ - ½ tsp. ground cayenne, depending on how spicy you like it
1 or 2 sprigs cilantro
1 sprig fresh thyme
Salt & pepper to taste

Roast Eggplant: If using whole cumin seeds, toast until fragrant in skillet. Grind in mortar and pestle or with coffee grinder. Preheat oven to 400 degrees. Place eggplant (sliced lengthwise) on a baking sheet, brush lightly with olive oil, then rub with ground cumin seeds. Roast for about a half-hour, or until eggplant can be pierced easily with a fork. Cool slightly, then remove eggplant meat from skin, and set aside.

Soup: In a large soup pot, heat 2-3 tablespoons olive oil over medium-low heat, add onions and cook until soft. Add chopped celery and continue to cook, stirring occasionally, until soft. Pour in 1-2 cups chicken stock. Add diced tomatoes, garlic, cilantro, parsley, thyme and eggplant. Add just enough stock to cover the surface of the contents of the soup (you can always add more stock later to thin down, if necessary). Season with ground cayenne, salt & pepper. Bring soup to a low simmer and cook for 20-25 minutes.

In batches, blend soup until smooth. Place soup back in pot and reheat to serve. Adjust seasonings. For pretties, garnish with cilantro leaves.

Custardy Eggplant Parmesan

I love eggplant but hate that nearly every recipe calls for frying it in oil. Consequently, my eggplant was starting to pile up, so I decided to come up with an alternative that still tastes good but doesn't require all that extra oil. I'm telling you, this is sublime! Nowhere near as heavy as the typical eggplant Parmesan, and great the next day, too. Feel free to ad lib; the amounts here are approximate.

Olive oil spray (I have a spritzer but PAM makes an olive oil spray that works great)
About 2 lbs. or less of eggplant, UNPEELED, sliced in about ½-inch thick rounds
½ cup ricotta cheese
2 large eggs
½ cup evaporated milk (or half and half)
1 generous cup of grated Parmesan
Salt and pepper
1 cup of spaghetti sauce (yours or out of a jar)
Optional: 1 link of Italian style sausage – I used the vegan variety

Preheat the oven to 400 degrees F.

After slicing the eggplant, spray it lightly with olive oil and cook on a grill pan or hot griddle for a few minutes, until slices are cooked through. Be sure to flip them over to get both sides browned. I used my large grill pan and still had to cook the eggplant in two batches.

Meanwhile, in a small bowl, mix together the ricotta, egg, evaporated milk, ½ cup of the Parmesan, about a ¼ teaspoon salt and several grinds of black pepper.

Optional: If you are using the sausage, go ahead and brown it in a separate skillet, breaking it into small bits. Add to the spaghetti sauce.

In a casserole dish, layer half the eggplant slices, then sprinkle with a handful of Parmesan, S&P, half the spaghetti sauce and half the ricotta mixture. Add the second layer of eggplant, another good sprinkle of Parmesan, S&P and the rest of the spaghetti sauce and ricotta mixture. Sprinkle a little more Parmesan on top and bake for 25 or 30 minutes or until the custard sets and the top is browned.

Ritzy Oven-baked Eggplant Parmesan

My sister in Chicago is an amazing cook, and I have her to thank for quite a few recipes. Here is one of hers — easy and really good. Her recipe is for two generous, meal-size portions, but it's easy enough to double. A big advantage over the usual eggplant Parmesan is that this is not a bit oily because there's nothing fried. It's much lighter on the calories, but just as tasty.

1 (8oz) package Ritz crackers
1 tsp. onion powder
1 tsp. black pepper
1 tsp. garlic powder
Scant ½ tsp. salt
2 eggs, beaten
½ lime, juiced
1 eggplant, peeled and sliced into ½ inch rounds
¾ cup freshly grated Parmesan cheese
Tomato sauce (your own or from a jar)
Optional: 2 slices mozzarella

Preheat oven to 375. Spray baking sheet with cooking spray or lightly grease with olive oil.

Crumble crackers into a large bowl. Stir in onion powder, pepper, garlic powder and salt. In a separate bowl, stir together eggs and lime juice. Dip eggplant slices into egg mixture, then dredge in cracker mix, and place on a baking sheet.

Bake for 15 minutes. Turn eggplant pieces, top with grated cheese, and cook an additional 15 minutes. To serve, top with tomato sauce and, if desired, also with a piece of mozzarella and put in oven or under broiler to melt cheese.

Kohlrabi

*Kohlrabi, with their twirling upper stems, always put me in mind of little space
aliens. The odd shape notwithstanding, kohlrabi is a crispy, tasty vegetable when
you eat it raw — a very nice addition to salads. Just be sure to peel the thick
outer skin.*

Kohlrabi Home Fries

A couple or three kohlrabi
A tablespoon or so of flour
Salt
A couple tablespoons of vegetable oil, or more as needed
Chili powder, ground cumin, curry powder, paprika or other spice, to suit
  your taste

Peel the thick outer skin of the kohlrabi and cut into thick sticks, French-fry
style. Heat the oil over medium-high heat in a heavy skillet (cast iron is good).
Meanwhile, place the flour in a large bowl, season with salt and quickly toss
the kohlrabi sticks in the flour to lightly coat.

When the oil is rippling, carefully add the kohlrabi to the pan in batches so
that the pan isn't crowded. Cook on one side until browned, about 2 to 3
minutes, then turn to brown on the other side for another 2 to 3 minutes.
The procedure should take only about 5 minutes if there is enough oil in the
pan. Drain on paper towels, then sprinkle right away with the seasoning of
your choice. Serve hot.

Tomatoes

Probably my favorite time in the garden is when the tomatoes are finally getting ripe. All those beautiful and delicious heirloom varieties just make my mouth water. So who needs lots of recipes for those? Here is one offering for early tomatoes; look in the late-season chapter for other great tomato sauces.

Roasted Tomato Sauce

This is one of the most delectable tomato sauces I've ever eaten, and so simple. It's great on pasta or smeared on crusty bread as an appetizer.

About 3 pounds of plum-style tomatoes, quartered
Extra virgin olive oil
6-8 cloves garlic, chopped
½ cup Parmesan
½ cup bread crumbs
S&P, parsley, oregano and basil to taste

Use a large roasting pan. Cover bottom with olive oil. Add chopped garlic and tomatoes. Salt tomatoes, then toss in the oil. Cover with the cheese/herbs/breadcrumbs mixture, and bake 30 minutes at 375. Stir all together and return to the oven for another 30 minutes.

This makes a thick and amazingly flavorful sauce, which you can thin with water or a little wine.

Potatoes – White and Sweet

Sweet Potatoes with Bleu Cheese & Bacon Appetizers

3 large sweet potatoes, unpeeled, cut into ¼ inch rounds and tossed with:
 garlic salt, black pepper, smoked paprika, thyme and just enough olive oil to get the spices to stick to the potato slices
8 oz. cooked & crumbled bacon

8 oz. bleu cheese, crumbled
Chives, snipped for garnish

Pre-heat oven to 425°F with rack(s) in middle. Toss sweet potatoes with olive oil and seasonings. Arrange in a single layer on baking sheet(s). Bake for about 25-30 minutes until sweet potatoes are golden brown & softened. Take potatoes out of oven, put rack in lower half of the oven and set temperature to low broil. Top each sweet potato round with blue cheese and bacon crumbles. Broil until the cheese is bubbling & melted. Let cool in baking sheets & top with snipped chives. Serve warm or at room temperature.

White and Sweet Potato Gratin with Fresh Herbs
This is a fabulous Thanksgiving or Christmas side dish for lots of people – serves 12.

1 ½ lbs. white or yellow potatoes
1 ½ lbs. sweet potatoes
2 cups light cream
½ stick butter
2 garlic cloves, minced
1 T. minced fresh parsley
1 T. minced fresh rosemary
1 T. minced fresh sage
1 T. minced fresh thyme
1 ½ tsp. fine sea salt
¾ tsp. freshly ground black pepper
5 oz. grated Gruyere

Fill large bowl with cold water. Working with 1 potato at a time, peel, then cut into 1/8-inch-thick rounds and place in bowl with water. Repeat with sweet potatoes. Combine cream, butter, and garlic in medium saucepan; bring to simmer. Remove from heat. Mix all herbs in small bowl. Mix sea salt and black pepper in another small bowl.

Butter 13x9x2-inch glass baking dish. Drain potatoes, then pat dry with kitchen towels. Transfer half of potatoes to prepared baking dish. Use hands to distribute and spread evenly. Sprinkle with half of salt-pepper mixture, then half of herb mixture. Sprinkle with half of cheese. Repeat with remaining potatoes, salt-pepper mixture, herb mixture, and cheese. Pour cream mixture over gratin, pressing lightly to submerge potato mixture as much as possible. DO AHEAD: *Can be made 6 hours ahead.* Cover with plastic wrap and chill. Remove plastic wrap before baking.

Preheat oven to 400°F. Cover gratin tightly with foil. Bake 30 minutes. Uncover; bake until top of gratin is golden and most of liquid is absorbed, about 25 minutes longer. Let stand 10 minutes; serve.

Causa

Pronounced COW-sa, a Peruvian dish I learned from my husband. A favorite summertime recipe, it takes a little work but it's worth it. All quantities are approximate; don't be afraid to fiddle with the ingredients. Be bold! Don't hesitate over the lemon juice or the olive oil. Life is short…

6 medium potatoes
½ cup minced onion
1/3 cup fresh lemon or lime juice (I use a combination)
1 tsp. fresh hot chile, finely chopped, or to taste
Cayenne pepper to taste
1/3 cup olive oil
Salt

Mayonnaise (or Vegannaise)
2 ripe avocados
2-3 tomatoes
1 can albacore tuna in water, drained (optional)
Salt and pepper to taste

Peel and boil the potatoes. Once cooked, drain off water and mash down thoroughly. Make a sauce with the next six ingredients and add to the mashed potatoes. Mix well, and taste to correct seasoning. (I like it with a good citrus tang.)

In a casserole place a third of the mashed potatoes and spread lightly with mayonnaise/vegannaise. On top, distribute the tuna if using, then cover with slices of tomato; season with salt and pepper. Cover with another third of the potato, lightly coat with mayo, add sliced avocados, season with s&p, and cover with a final layer of potato. Cover with plastic wrap and chill for a couple of hours, or until dish is cold. Serve in squares (like lasagna) on a bed of lettuce.

Papas a la Huancaína (Huancayo-Style Potatoes)

This is a first course or salad dish. The sauce is actually made with Peruvian queso fresco, but since it is not available here, I combine cream cheese and feta to achieve a similar taste and consistency.

2 lbs. fingerlings or new potatoes
1 package cream cheese
About 8 ounces of feta cheese
1 small cooked potato
2 hard-boiled egg yolks
About 2-3 tsp. of Ají Amarillo* paste, or other hot pepper to taste
About 1/4 – 1/3 cup evaporated milk or ½ and ½
About ¼ cup olive oil
Juice of 1 lemon

Wash and boil potatoes in their skins until tender; drain and cool.

Put all remaining ingredients into a blender and process until sauce is smooth. If the mixture is too stiff, add a little more milk and/or olive oil. You want it thick and creamy, not runny. Taste it – if necessary add more aji or lemon juice. It doesn't usually need any extra salt, since the feta is pretty salty.

On a platter arrange lettuce leaves, then put the boiled potatoes on top, and pour the huancaína sauce over the potatoes. You can also do individual plates.

Bonus! You can also use the sauce as a dip for fried yucca or tortilla chips. If using yucca, peel the root, then boil it whole until it pierces easily with a fork – same as a potato. Cool, then cut into sticks. There is a tough fiber running down the center of the root – it's best to remove that. Brown in a little oil in a frying pan, then dip into the sauce. Delicioso.

* Note: Ají Amarillo paste is available in some Latin groceries. The chile is native to Peru and has more flavor than heat. If you can't find it, you can substitute some finely minced jalapeño or other hot fresh chile.

Fennel and Potato Bake
Serves 6

1 ½ T. butter, plus more for pan
2 medium fennel bulbs, (about 1 lb.)
1 ½ lbs. potatoes, peeled
Coarse salt and ground pepper
½ cup plus 6 T. grated Asiago cheese
½ cup heavy cream

Preheat oven to 400 degrees. Lightly butter an 8-inch square baking dish. Trim fennel bulbs; halve, and core. Slice bulbs and potatoes very thin (1/8 inch thick). Add potatoes to prepared dish in three layers, alternating with layers of fennel; season each layer with salt and pepper, sprinkle with 2 tablespoons Asiago, and dot with 1/2 tablespoon butter. (Omit cheese from final layer.) Pour cream over top. Bake until potatoes are tender when pierced with the tip of a paring knife, about 45 minutes. Sprinkle with remaining ½ cup grated Asiago; bake until golden brown, 15 to 20 minutes.

Chicken

Field 51 Roasted Chicken with Basil, Potatoes and Tomatoes
(Adapted from Jamie Oliver)

One whole chicken, cut up (or equivalent in pieces)
Sea salt and fresh pepper
A big bunch of basil, leaves picked and stems chopped
2 big handfuls cherry tomatoes
2 whole bulbs garlic, separated into cloves but *unpeeled*
1 fresh red chile (or a sprinkling of dried chile)
Olive oil
2 big handfuls of fingerlings or new potatoes, scrubbed

Preheat the oven to 350. Season chicken pieces and put them in a snug-fitting pan in one layer. (A Dutch oven is perfect.) Throw on all the basil leaves and stalks, tomatoes and potatoes, tucking the tomatoes underneath. Scatter the garlic cloves with the chopped chili and drizzle with olive oil. Bake 1½ hours, until chicken skin is crisp. Can't beat it.

Basic Stir-Fry with Chicken and CSA Basket Veggies
Will serve 6 generously
There are about a million stir-fry recipes, which should give you great comfort: Stir-fry is impossible to mess up if you just follow a few simple rules. You can use just about any vegetable you like, too, which makes it the perfect dish for your weekly veggie basket. Here are the rules: 1) Chop everything before you start cooking; 2) Keep the heat high to cook the food quickly and keep it from getting soggy; and 3) Cook the tenderest vegetables last. It's not necessary to use a wok – a large pot or deep skillet will do. For a vegetarian dish, just leave out the chicken.

½-1 lb. raw chicken, cut into bite-size pieces
1 tsp. cornstarch
1 T. rice wine
Splash of soy sauce or Braggs
A little bit of fresh grated ginger

1-2 T. vegetable oil
2-3 cloves garlic, minced
A chunk of fresh ginger, peeled and diced (~ 2 T)
A fresh hot chile, seeded and minced (or a good pinch of crushed red pepper)
2 carrots, peeled and sliced on the diagonal
2 stalks celery, sliced on the diagonal
A couple handfuls of cauliflower, broken into small florets
4-5 green onions, chopped (green and white parts)
Handful of peanuts
4 or 5 handfuls of tatsoi
1-2 tsp. sesame oil
1 tsp. sesame seeds
3-4 T. soy sauce or Bragg's
About ½ cup chicken or veg broth mixed with 1 tsp. cornstarch

(If you are not using chicken, skip to the next paragraph): In a small bowl, toss the chicken pieces with the cornstarch, rice wine, soy sauce and ginger and let it sit while you chop all your vegetables.

Chop all your vegetables. Heat the wok or pot on high heat, then add a tablespoon of oil. When it shimmers, add chicken (if using) and stir quickly for a couple of minutes; remove with a slotted spoon and set aside. Add in another tablespoon of oil if needed, then add the garlic, ginger and chili and stir for about a minute. Add the carrots and celery and stir for a minute, then add the cauliflower and cook, stirring for 3 or 4 minutes. Add in the peanuts, green onions and tatsoi, stirring until tatsoi just begins to wilt. Finally, add the sesame oil and seeds, soy sauce and broth mixed with cornstarch, and add the chicken back in. Mix well and stir until the sauce thickens. Taste and adjust seasonings, and serve over rice or noodles.

Whole Roasted Chicken Made Easy

I would love to stake a claim for this recipe (actually a bunch of recipes in one), but it comes from my favorite cookbook writer, Mark Bittman. If you haven't discovered him, do yourself a favor. His How to Cook Everything *is simply fantastic (and very easy to follow), and his more recent book,* The Food Matters Cookbook, *is perfect for a vegetable CSA, as his focus is on plant foods, using meat and seafood primarily as seasoning. Here is his one recipe with actually 11 different variations, all of them delicious.*

Simplest Whole Roast Chicken Six Ways
Time: About 1 hour

1 whole chicken, 3 to 4 pounds, trimmed of excess fat
3 T. extra virgin olive oil
Salt and freshly ground black pepper
A few sprigs fresh tarragon, rosemary, or thyme (optional)
5 or 6 cloves garlic, peeled (optional)
Chopped fresh herbs for garnish

Heat the oven to 450°F. Five minutes after turning on the oven, put a cast-iron or other heavy ovenproof skillet on a rack set low in the oven. Rub the chicken with the olive oil, sprinkle it with salt and pepper, and put the herb sprigs on it if you're using them.

When both oven and pan are hot, 10 or 15 minutes later, carefully put the chicken, breast side up, in the hot skillet; if you're using garlic, scatter it around the bird. Roast, undisturbed, for 40 to 50 minutes or until an instant-read thermometer inserted in the meaty part of the thigh registers 155–165°F. Tip the pan to let the juices from the bird's cavity flow into the pan (if they are red, cook for another 5 minutes). Transfer the bird to a platter and let it rest; if you like, pour the pan juices into a clear measuring cup, then pour or spoon off some of the fat. Reheat the juices if necessary, quarter the bird, garnish, and serve with the pan juices.

Herb-Roasted Chicken
A little more elegant: Start the cooking without the olive oil. About halfway

through, spoon a mixture of ¼ cup olive oil and 2 tablespoons chopped fresh parsley, chervil, basil, or dill over the chicken. Garnish with more chopped herbs.

Lemon-Roasted Chicken

Brush the chicken with olive oil before roasting; cut a lemon in half and put it in the chicken's cavity. Roast, more or less undisturbed, until done; squeeze the juice from the cooked lemon over the chicken and carve.

Roast Chicken with Paprika

With good paprika, quite delicious: Combine the olive oil with about 1 T. sweet paprika or smoked pimentón.

Roast Chicken with Soy Sauce.

Chinese-style roast chicken, made easy: Replace the olive oil with peanut or neutral oil, like grapeseed or corn. Halfway through the cooking, spoon or brush over the chicken a mixture of ¼ cup soy sauce, 2 T. honey, 1 tsp. minced garlic, 1 tsp. grated or minced fresh ginger (or 1 tsp. ground ginger), and ¼ cup minced scallion.

Roast Chicken with Cumin, Honey, and Orange Juice

Sweet and exotic: Halfway through the cooking, spoon or brush over the chicken a mixture of 2 T. freshly squeezed orange juice, 2 T. honey, 1 tsp. minced garlic, 2 tsp. ground cumin, and salt and pepper to taste.

4 More Ways to Flavor Simplest Whole Roast Chicken

There are many ways to flavor a roast chicken; here are some simple ideas to get you started:

1. Lemon: Use 3 T. freshly squeezed lemon juice in addition to or in place of olive oil.

2. Lime: Use 3 T. freshly squeezed lime juice in a soy sauce mix (as in the Roast Chicken with Soy Sauce variation) or with some minced jalapeño or serrano chiles or hot red pepper flakes, chopped fresh cilantro leaves to taste, and a tablespoon or two of peanut oil.

3. Honey-Mustard: Combine 2 T. to 1/3 cup mustard with 2 T. honey and rub the chicken with this mixture during the final stages of roasting.

4. Wine: Put ½ cup white wine and 2 cloves crushed garlic in the bottom of the roasting pan; baste with this in addition to or in place of the olive oil mixture.

Chapter 4

Autumn harvest: Warming food for cool days

There's something a little wistful about the end of the season, as the summer crops die back and the fall harvest beckons. There is still plenty of life left in the garden, though, and much comfort to be derived from warm meals on brisk evenings!

Apples

Elsa Gebhardt's German-Swiss Apple Cake

My grandmother emigrated from the Alsace region to Boston when she was a little girl. This is one of her mother's recipes, so it must be very old: my gran would be 100+ if she were still around.

Mix together:
1 cup sugar
1 cup flour
½ tsp. baking powder
Pinch salt
2 eggs

Then add:
2+ cups tart chopped apples (don't chop too small)
½ cup chopped walnuts
1 tsp. vanilla

Turn into a small greased cake pan and bake at 375 for about 35 – 45 minutes.

Broccoli

Easy Oven Roasted Broccoli with Garlic, Lemon & Parmesan

About 1½ lbs. broccoli crowns, cut into bite-sized florets
Olive oil
4 cloves garlic, minced
Zest of half a lemon
½ cup freshly grated Parmesan
Lemon wedges, to serve.

Preheat the oven to 450F. In a large bowl, add the broccoli florets, drizzle liberally with olive oil and toss to coat. Add the lemon zest and garlic, and toss again until well mixed. Spread the broccoli on a large baking sheet in a single layer and roast in the oven for 10 minutes.

Sprinkle with Parmesan and return to the oven until the Parmesan begins to bubble and the broccoli is tender and golden around the edges, about a further 10 minutes.

Serve with lemon wedges (or squeeze a little of the lemon juice over just before serving).

Parmesan-Roasted Broccoli

4 to 5 pounds broccoli
4 garlic cloves, peeled and thinly sliced
Good olive oil
1 ½ tsp. kosher salt
½ tsp. freshly ground black pepper
2 tsp. grated lemon zest
2 T. freshly squeezed lemon juice
3 T. pine nuts, toasted
1/3 cup freshly grated Parmesan cheese
2 T. julienned fresh basil leaves (about 12 leaves)

Preheat the oven to 425 degrees F. Cut the broccoli florets from the thick stalks, leaving an inch or two of stalk attached to the florets, discarding the rest of the stalks. Cut the larger pieces through the base of the head with a small knife, pulling the florets apart. You should have about 8 cups of florets. Place the broccoli florets on a sheet pan large enough to hold them in a single layer. Toss the garlic on the broccoli and drizzle with 5 tablespoons olive oil. Sprinkle with the salt and pepper. Roast for 20 to 25 minutes, until crisp-tender and the tips of some of the florets are browned.

Remove the broccoli from the oven and immediately toss with 1 ½ tablespoons olive oil, the lemon zest, lemon juice, pine nuts, Parmesan, and basil. Serve hot.

Celery

The nice leafy tops of celery make for wonderful seasoning in soup stock, dried and combined with salt for seasoning, or as celery pesto. I also like to bake the celery — a different sort of side dish.

Celery and Zucchini Pancakes

About 1 cup shredded zucchini
About 1 cup minced celery, previously blanched
A little bit of minced onion
1 large clove garlic, minced
½ cup flour
½ cup panko breadcrumbs
1 tsp. salt
Several twists of fresh ground black pepper
1 egg
About ¼ cup Parmesan cheese
Splash of milk

Clean celery and blanch in boiling water for about 5 minutes; drain, cool and mince.

Mix all ingredients, adding just enough milk to hold the mixture together. Heat a griddle and lightly rub with oil. When griddle is hot, reduce heat to medium or medium low. Put batter on the griddle in generous spoonsful and flatten. When browned on the bottom, flip, flatten, then cover with a lid, checking occasionally to make sure they don't burn. I flipped these a couple times. They take about 5-6 minutes to cook. Delicious.

Homemade Celery Salt

Line a microwave-safe plate with a paper towel and arrange celery leaves in a single layer. Cover with another paper towel and zap in 30-second increments until the leaves are brittle (maybe a couple of minutes). Cool the leaves, then rub them through a sieve over a dish of salt, and mix. Or, you can grind the leaves and salt together if you have a spice grinder. Great seasoning for eggs, fish or rimming a glass of your favorite icy libation.

Celery Leaf Pesto

Great on pasta, of course, but also spread on sandwich bread instead of mayonnaise.

About 3 cups of celery leaves and thin stems, roughly chopped
2 cloves garlic
½ cup toasted almonds or walnuts
Squeeze of fresh lemon or lime juice
Olive oil – to desired consistency, but probably 4-5 T.
About 1/3 cup grated Parmesan cheese

Toast the almonds or walnuts in a dry skillet over medium heat, tossing until fragrant and lightly browned. Cool for a few minutes, then put in the blender, along with garlic, celery leaves/stems and citrus juice. Begin to process, gradually adding in olive oil until you reach the consistency you like. Transfer to a small bowl, mix in Parmesan cheese by hand, then taste and add salt if needed.

Baked Celery

So easy. Trim your celery ends, cut the stalks in half lengthwise, and lay them into a lightly greased baking dish. Make your favorite white sauce (butter, flour, milk, S&P, a little nutmeg), add in some grated cheese (any kind that you have on hand), pour over the celery and maybe sprinkle some panko breadcrumbs on top. Bake at 350, covered for the first 20 minutes, then uncovered until the stalks are tender and it's all bubbly and browning. Yum.

They're only ugly on the outside: Late-season tomatoes

Harvesting tomatoes late in the season is really like going on a treasure hunt — the weight of the fruit pulls the plants over, vines get tangled up on the ground, and some of the best tomatoes lurk behind layers of overlapping leaves (and spider webs), well hidden from view. I actually find the quirky shape of many October tomatoes amusing and kind of sweet — the Charlie Brown Christmas tree of heirloom tomatoes. Red-on-one-side-green-on-the-other coloration, lumpy shapes, often split skins that have scarred over make them homely on the outside, but they are just as beautiful on the inside. And, they make the most wonder tomato sauce. Besides, it's easy. There are loads of different ways of making sauce, but here's how I do it. There's usually a supply of hard green tomatoes, too — fruits that just won't ripen in the cool air and short days of autumn.

Easy Fresh Tomato Sauce

A dozen tomatoes, more or less
One good-sized onion, chopped
Several cloves of garlic, minced
2 good stalks of celery, chopped
Olive oil
A couple of small carrots, finely minced or grated
Fresh herbs if you have any (basil, oregano, rosemary) or dried if you don't
Salt and pepper to taste
Optional:
A generous splash of red wine
Some grated Parmesan cheese

Prepare your tomatoes. If I have the time, I peel and seed them (some say the seeds cause the sauce to be bitter). If I don't, I just core them, cut away any uglies, and chop them up.

In a large pot, heat a tablespoon or two of olive oil, then add the onion, garlic and celery and sauté over medium heat about 10 minutes. Add in the tomatoes, carrots (which take away any acidity), herbs, S&P, and cook at a low simmer. Every once in awhile, mash the tomatoes down with a potato masher to get some of the lumps out. Depending on how juicy your tomatoes are and how thick or thin you like your sauce, you can let your sauce bubble away until it reaches the thickness you like. The longer the sauce simmers, the deeper the flavor. On the other hand, a sauce that is cooked for less time will have more of that fresh tomato flavor.

I do like to add in a good glug of red wine and some Parmesan cheese towards the end of cooking; just adds a nice zing. You can use the sauce as is, or you can add other goodies to it – browned Italian sausage, mushrooms, green peppers…you get the idea. **Note**: I actually like my sauce kind of chunky/lumpy, but if you have picky eaters, you can zip it in the blender for just a few seconds.

Raw Green Tomato Salsa

3 or 4 green tomatoes
2 or 3 peppers (a variety of colors and 'heats' according to your personal
 preference)
½ medium red onion
2 or 3 cloves garlic
Generous tablespoon each of chopped cilantro and chopped parsley
Juice of 1 lime
Scant ¼ cup vinegar
Salt and pepper to taste
Sugar or agave to taste

Finely chop the tomatoes, peppers, onions and garlic. Mix them together with the remaining ingredients, and let it sit for at least 30 minutes before serving so all the flavors marinate and blend. Taste and adjust seasonings, then enjoy!

Cooked Green Tomato Salsa Verde
Use fresh or freeze for later use; recipe can easily be doubled or tripled

2 pounds firm, green tomatoes, cored and quartered
1 medium onion, coarsely chopped
1 fresh green Anaheim or other large, mildly-flavored chile pepper, stem and
seeds removed, quartered
3-4 green jalapeño chiles (for a medium-hot salsa), stems removed, quartered
3 garlic cloves, coarsely chopped
1 tsp. sea salt
¼ tsp. ground cumin
1 T. olive oil
3 T. water
½ tsp. fresh lemon zest

1 T. fresh lemon juice
1 tsp. honey or sugar
1/3 cup loosely packed cilantro leaves, coarsely chopped

Combine the green tomatoes, onion, chile peppers, garlic, salt, cumin, olive oil and water in a stock pot. Bring to a boil and cook covered on a medium-low heat burner for about 10 minutes, stirring occasionally. Add more water only if needed to maintain the most minimal broth. Stir in and simmer for an additional five minutes the lemon zest, lemon juice, honey (or sugar) and cilantro. Taste and adjust the seasoning if needed by adding more lemon juice, honey and/or salt, to taste. Spoon the mixture (in batches) into a blender and pulse until the salsa reaches the consistency you prefer, either chunky or a smooth puree. Makes about one quart of salsa, which should be stored in the refrigerator or freezer.

Green Tomato and Chard Gratin
Serves 6; can be made ahead and reheated

1 bunch chard
1 lb. green tomatoes, sliced about 1/3-inch thick
½ cup cornmeal for dredging
Salt and pepper to taste
3 T. olive oil
1 medium onion, chopped
2 garlic cloves, minced
2 tsp. fresh thyme leaves, chopped
3 large eggs, beaten
½ cup milk
3 oz. Gruyere cheese, grated (½ cup, tightly packed)

Preheat the oven to 375 degrees. Oil a 2-quart baking dish. Bring a large pot of generously salted water to a boil, and fill a bowl with ice water. Wash the chard and add to the boiling water; blanch for about a minute, drain and transfer to ice water. Cool, then squeeze out excess water and chop.

Season the sliced tomatoes and the cornmeal lightly with salt and pepper. Dredge the tomatoes in the cornmeal. Heat 2 tablespoons of olive oil in a heavy nonstick skillet over medium-high heat, and fry the tomatoes for a minute or two on each side, just until lightly colored. Remove from the heat and set aside.

Heat the remaining tablespoon of olive oil over medium heat in the skillet in which you cooked the tomatoes, add the onion and cook, stirring, until tender, about five minutes. Add a generous pinch of salt and the garlic, and cook together for another minute, until the garlic is fragrant. Add the thyme and the chopped chard, and stir together for a minute over medium heat. Season to taste with salt and pepper.

Beat the eggs in a large bowl with ½ tsp. salt and freshly ground pepper to taste. Whisk in the milk. Stir in the cheese and the chard mixture. Transfer to the gratin dish. Layer the tomatoes over the top. Place in the oven, and bake 30 to 40 minutes, until set and beginning to brown.

Winter Squash

It's a pumpkin, it's a cushaw, it's delicious any way you cook it. It is Fall, after all, and time for pumpkins, cushaws, butternuts and hubbards. Many winter squashes can be used interchangeably. And the really nice thing is that winter squashes of all varieties will keep for a long time if you store them in a cool, dark place. Plus, you can freeze the pulp once you cook and mash it. Just bring it out another day for a Thanksgiving pumpkin pie or a pot of pumpkin soup. Here's the bonus: The seeds make a fabulous snack. Just clean off the fibers, toss the seeds with a little olive oil and salt, spread out on a cookie sheet and bake at 375 until they are golden.

Roasted Pumpkin with Shallots

Eat the pumpkin just as you would a wedge of melon, scooping out the cooked flesh with a spoon or fork. If you prefer, peel the skin before roasting.

1 (3-pound) pumpkin, seeded and cut into 8 wedges
6 large shallots, peeled and quartered
6 cloves garlic, thinly sliced
1/3 cup olive oil
2 T. balsamic vinegar
1 T. chopped fresh oregano
1 T. sliced, fresh sage leaves
2 tsp. kosher salt
1 tsp. coarse-ground pepper

Preheat oven to 425 degrees F. Combine the pumpkin, shallots, and garlic in a roasting pan and set aside. Combine the remaining ingredients in a small bowl, pour the mixture over the pumpkin, and toss to coat. Roast, turning the vegetables twice during cooking, until browned and tender, about an hour.

Mark Bittman's Pureed Butternut Squash with Ginger

1 ½ lbs. butternut or other winter squash, peeled and cut into chunks
2 T. butter
1 to 2 tsp. peeled and roughly chopped fresh ginger or 1 tsp. ground ginger
Salt and freshly ground black pepper to taste
1 tsp. brown sugar, or to taste, optional

Place squash in a steamer above about 1 inch of salted water. Cover and cook until the squash is very tender, about 20 minutes.

While it is still hot, place the squash in the container of a food processor with the butter and ginger; process until smooth. Taste and add salt, pepper, and brown sugar if you like. Reheat over low heat or in a microwave and serve.

Other flavorings for Pureed Squash:
1. A small handful of fresh herbs, including parsley, cilantro, mint, and sage.
2. Maple syrup or honey in place of brown sugar.
3. Olive oil in place of butter.
4. Other ground spices in place of ginger, including cardamom, cinnamon, mace, and nutmeg.
5. A seeded jalapeno pepper

Pumpkin Biscuits
Serve with thin slices of country ham!

4 cups flour
2 ½ T. baking powder
1 tsp. salt
2 tsp. ginger
½ tsp. cayenne pepper
1 cup (2 sticks) unsalted butter, chilled
1 ½ cups pumpkin purée
1 T. honey
½ cup buttermilk

Preheat oven to 400 degrees F. Combine flour, baking powder, salt, ginger, and cayenne in a large bowl. Cut the chilled butter into small pieces and cut the butter into the flour mixture using a pastry cutter, two knives, or your hands until the mixture resembles coarse meal. Set aside. Combine the pumpkin purée and honey in a small bowl. Add the pumpkin mixture to the flour mixture and stir until just combined. Add the buttermilk and stir just until mixture clings together and is combined.

Lightly coat a baking sheet with vegetable oil and set aside. Turn the biscuit dough out onto a lightly floured surface and knead about 10 times. Roll the dough out to 3/4-inch thickness, cut biscuits out with a 3 1/2-inch round cutter, gather the scraps, gently press together, and repeat until all of the dough is used. Place biscuits 1 inch apart on the prepared baking sheet and bake until golden -- 25 to 30 minutes. Transfer to a wire rack to cool.

Pumpkin Chowder
Serves 8

3 T. olive oil
2 leeks, trimmed of tough green tops and chopped
3 garlic cloves, finely chopped
2 bell peppers, chopped
2 ¼ lbs. pumpkin, peeled, seeded, and cut into 1/2- by 1-inch-thick pieces
1 ½ tsp. chopped fresh marjoram
¼ tsp. crushed red pepper
2 bay leaves
¼ tsp. salt
¼ tsp. black pepper
1¼ cups frozen corn
6 cups vegetable broth

Heat olive oil in a large pot or Dutch oven over medium heat. Add leeks and cook until very soft, about 5 minutes. Add garlic and cook for about 2 minutes. Stir in green peppers, reduce heat to medium-low, and cook until peppers soften, about 8 more minutes. Add the remaining ingredients and cook until pumpkin is tender, about 30 minutes.

Thai-style Butternut Squash Soup
Serves 6

2-3 T. olive oil
2 medium carrots, diced
2 small ribs celery, diced
1 medium apple, diced
1 medium onion, diced
1 T. chopped fresh ginger
4 cups peeled and cubed butternut squash (about 1 medium)
1-2 T. red curry paste (to your taste; I like it spicy)
½ tsp. chopped fresh thyme
4 - 6 cups veg. or chicken broth
½ cup coconut milk
Sea salt & ground black pepper
Fresh cilantro, chopped

In a large soup kettle, heat olive oil, then add carrot, celery, apple, onion and ginger. Cook until veggies begin to soften and onion turns translucent. Stir in squash, curry paste and thyme, then add broth and coconut milk, and season with salt and pepper. Bring to a boil, reduce heat and simmer until squash is fork-tender, about 30 minutes.

Let the soup cool slightly before blending. Blend in batches and puree until smooth. Serve soup with a garnish of chopped fresh cilantro.

Easy and Basic Pumpkin Soup
Serves 6

Olive oil
1 onion, diced
2 T. chopped fresh ginger
3 cloves garlic, minced
2 or 2 ½ lbs. pumpkin, peeled, seeded and cut into chunks
Salt and pepper to taste
A little fresh thyme or marjoram, chopped (or use a pinch of dry)
4 or 5 cups of broth – chicken or vegetable

In a large pot heat a good drizzle of olive oil over medium heat, then add in the onion and ginger and sauté, stirring, for a couple of minutes, until the onion starts to soften. Add in the garlic and stir til just fragrant, then add the pumpkin, seasonings and broth. Bring to a low simmer and cook for 20 – 30 minutes, or until the pumpkin is soft. Cool slightly, then puree in batches in the blender until smooth and creamy. Taste and adjust seasonings, then reheat and serve.

Roasted Pumpkin Soup #1

4 cups peeled cubed pumpkin
1 large yellow onion, minced
6 cups chicken broth
2 cups heavy cream
4 T. butter
1 T. fresh Thyme
salt and freshly ground pepper
1/2 tsp. mace
1/4 tsp. cayenne pepper
1 T. minced garlic
1 bay leaf
2 T. olive oil

Preheat oven to 350 F. In a medium bowl toss pumpkin with olive oil and salt and pepper. Cook for 45 minutes until soft, and set aside.

In a large heavy-bottomed stockpot melt butter and sauté over medium heat for 5 minutes. Add garlic, thyme, bay leaf and spices and cook for an additional 15 minutes. Add 4 cups of the chicken stock and 2 cups of cream. Simmer over low heat.

Place cooled pumpkin in food processor with reserved chicken stock (2 cups) and puree until smooth. Add pureed pumpkin to the soup, bring to a boil over medium heat. Reduce heat to low and simmer for 1 hour.

Roasted Pumpkin Soup #2

1 (4-pound) sugar baby pumpkin, roasted and mashed
1 T. olive oil
Kosher salt
Freshly ground black pepper
½ cup small-dice bacon (3 slices)
½ cup small-dice shallots
¼ cup dry sherry
2 cups stock or low-sodium chicken broth
2 cups water
1 ½ tsp. finely chopped fresh thyme leaves
¼ cup heavy cream

Place the bacon in a large, heavy-bottomed saucepan or Dutch oven over medium heat and cook until crispy and the fat is rendered, about 10 minutes. Remove with a slotted spoon to a small paper-towel-lined plate and set aside.

Add the shallots to the bacon fat, season with salt and pepper, and sauté until softened, about 4 minutes. Add the sherry and cook until reduced by half, about 2 minutes. Add the stock or broth, water, thyme, and reserved pumpkin and season with salt and pepper. Stir to combine, then bring to a simmer. Reduce the heat to low and simmer until the flavors have melded, about 10 minutes.

Using a blender, purée the soup in batches until smooth, removing the small cap from the blender lid (the pour lid) and covering the space with a kitchen towel (this allows steam from the hot soup to escape and prevents the blender lid from popping off). Place the blended soup in a clean saucepan. Stir in the cream and season with salt and pepper as needed. Serve garnished with the reserved bacon.

Roasted Pumpkin soup #3

1 (2-pound) pumpkin, halved and seeds removed
1 tsp. salt
¼ tsp. plus a pinch freshly ground black pepper
3 T. olive oil
2 tsp. ground cinnamon
1 tsp. ground allspice
¾ cup chopped onion

½ cup chopped carrot
¼ cup chopped celery
2 T. minced ginger
1 T. minced garlic
3 ½ cups chicken stock
½ cup heavy cream
3 T. pumpkin seed oil
15 to 20 small sage leaves, fried

Preheat the oven to 400 degrees F. Place the pumpkin cut side up on a parchment lined baking sheet. Season with 1/2 tsp. of the salt and 1/4 tsp. of the pepper. Invert to the cut side down, and drizzle with 1 T. of the olive oil. Place in the oven and roast until the skin is golden brown and the pumpkin is tender, 50 to 60 minutes. Remove from the oven and allow to cool. Once cool enough to handle, use a spoon to scoop the pumpkin flesh from its skin and set pumpkin aside until ready to use. Discard the skin.

Set a medium saucepan over medium-high heat. Add the remaining 2 T. of olive oil and, when hot, add the cinnamon and allspice and cook, stirring constantly, for 1 minute. Add the onions, carrots, celery, ginger and garlic to the pan and sauté, stirring occasionally, until lightly caramelized, 3 to 4 minutes. Add the chicken stock and reserved pumpkin to the pan and bring the stock to a boil. Reduce to a simmer and cook the soup for 15 to 20 minutes, or until the vegetables are soft.

Remove the soup from the heat and process with an immersion blender (*or in batches in a blender) until smooth. Season with the remaining 1/2 tsp. salt and pinch of pepper. Add the cream to the soup and stir to combine. To serve, place 1 cup of the soup in each of 6 warmed soup bowls. Drizzle 2 tsp. of the pumpkin seed oil in the bowl and garnish with a 2 or 3 fried sage leaves.

Pumpkin and Chicken Chowder
Serves 8

2 red bell peppers
2 jalapeño peppers
2 T. olive oil
1 ½ lbs. boneless, skinless chicken breasts, diced
3 leeks, white and light-green parts only
1 (about 2 lbs.) pumpkin, peeled, seeded, cut into 1-inch chunks
3 T. flour
2 tsp. ground cumin
1 tsp. chili powder
1 tsp. salt
½ tsp. fresh ground pepper
1 ear (1 cup) corn kernels
5 cups chicken broth
1 T. fresh oregano leaves
½ cup sour cream (optional)

Roast the peppers: Preheat oven to broil. Place the red peppers and jalapeños on a baking sheet and cook under the broiler, turning occasionally, until the skins blacken, about 10 minutes. Seal the charred peppers in a plastic bag for 10 to 12 minutes. Peel, stem, seed, and cut peppers into 1/2-inch pieces. Set aside.

Make the soup: Heat the olive oil in a large Dutch oven over medium-high heat. Add the chicken pieces and cook until browned. Remove the chicken and keep warm. Add the leeks and pumpkin and sauté for about 5 minutes. Add the flour, cumin, chili powder, salt, and pepper and cook for 1 to 2 minutes. Add the corn, peppers, chicken, broth, and oregano and bring the soup to a boil. Reduce heat to low and simmer, about 30 minutes. Garnish with sour cream if desired and serve hot.

INDEX OF RECIPES BY MAIN INGREDIENT

Eggs

Fennel

Garlic scapes

Kale

Kohlrabi

Pasta

Pattypan squash

Potatoes

Tomatoes
Basic Andaluz Gazpacho - 34
Cooked Green Tomato Salsa Verde - 69
Easy Fresh Tomato Sauce - 68
Field 51 Roasted Chicken with Basil, Potatoes and Tomatoes - 58
Green Bean and Tomato Salad - 46
Green Tomato and Chard Gratin - 70
Raw Green Tomato Salsa – 69
Roasted Tomato Sauce - 54
White Bean and Sausage Ragout with Tomatoes, Kale and Zucchini - 36

Turnip greens
Hot Wilted Greens - 28
Meatless Turnip Greens with a Kick - 28
Mess o' Greens Salad with Warm Pecan Dressing - 29
Sautéed Fresh Turnip Greens - 27

Zucchini
Celery and Zucchini Pancakes - 66
Easiest Stuffed Squash with Herbs and Goat Cheese - 41
Grilled Squash with Pesto - 41
Matchstick Summer Squash and Carrot Sauté - 40
Raw Veggie Salad #1 - 40
Raw Veggie Salad #2 - 40
Refrigerator Bread and Butter Pickles – 43
White Bean and Sausage Ragout with Tomatoes, Kale and Zucchini - 36
Zucchini "Crab" Cakes - 42
Zucchini Chips - 43

26125111R00049

Made in the USA
Charleston, SC
25 January 2014